AN OBEISANCE TO FROGS

PREVIOUS PUBLICATIONS

A Lioness at My Heels (Hands-On Books 2011)
Messages from the Bees (Modjaji, 2017)

An Obeisance to Frogs

NEW POEMS

Robin
Winckel-Mellish

ACKNOWLEDGEMENTS

Some of the poems here collected first appeared
in the following magazines:
Stanzas
McGregor Poetry Festival Anthology
New Coin
Writing from Home Anthology, Amsterdam

•

First published in 2022
by Hands-On Books,
an imprint of Modjaji Books
Cape Town, South Africa
www.modjajibooks.co.za

© Robin Winckel-Mellish 2022

ISBN 978-1-928215-90-5

All rights reserved.
No part of this book may be reproduced or transmitted in any form or by any
means, mechanical or electronic, including photocopying or recording, or be
stored in any information storage or retrieval system without prior written
permission from the publisher.

•

Cover artwork by Fabrizio Ruggiero
Design and typesetting by Liz Gowans

CONTENTS

PART ONE

The Swallows	11
An Obeisance to Frogs	12
Snake	13
Boulders Beach. Stony Point. Dassen Island.	14
We Came for the Whales	15
Two Birds	17
Aria	18
Earthward	19
Messenger	20
Oracle	21
On the Stoep	22
Encounter	23
The Iconic Southernmost Tip of Africa Builds a New Monument	24
Essence	25

PART TWO

Cicadas	29
Borderlines	30
Abandoned in Tuscany	31
Turning Point	32
Day in the Veluwe	33
The Garden Next Door	34
Chestnut in Winter	35

PART THREE

Sunday Morning in Paris	39
A Street in Amsterdam	40
It Will Happen	41
A Look at Love	42
Embrace	43
My Father's Heart	44
Ode to Legs	46
The Wife of my Ex	47
Image	48
A Child Plays	49

PART FOUR

Kaggen, the Thief of Time	53

For Philip, John and Georgina

PART ONE

The Swallows

A bone-dry summer, showing
the shine of bleached stone,
ostrich heads down, great
bird bundles, black and grey
ships on the horizon,
only the sound of wind
and the purr of ocean when
the breeze turned my way.
I sensed it coming, thunder,
then a few drops, slowly
descending the Overberg
onto the plains, and by
the end of afternoon,
rain soft and delicate,
as if forgotten how to fall,
and a flight of swallows
flying suddenly, fast as bullets
over the veld, darting, swooping,
chirping, a feeding frenzy as
tiny insects rose up in the damp.

And then, as if knowing
that the earth had opened,
the rain beat down,
the fragrance of bush
and earth: damp bark
and wet grass,
the swallows gone.

An Obeisance to Frogs

It's that time of the year, he says
as side by side we walk
in the warmth of a spring evening,

the frogs in a nearby pond
clustered in their choir,
their song a mantra to the living,

as if all that is not needed
has gone, and from this,
a bold, new sound has been born.

My animist heart walks
with the gods who watch
and wait, like the frogs,

shaping themselves from mud
and gold as they hop and slither,
jewel eyes that watch the world.

Snake

As lethal as love. Hooded gold,
it stood up and glittered
in the half dark. Forked tongue
flickering, our musk encroaching,
we were the pungi, the snake
a swaying reed of rancour.

I had called in a local, thought
the vanishing tail burrowed
in an old rug was harmless,
a solitary mole snake keeping
house in my garage, not
the spitting sleek silk

of a Cape cobra, potent
as a king, our terror now
too dense to breathe.
Over in seconds,
crushed and dislocated,
the terrible eye still flickering,

my heart a heavy hammer.

Boulders Beach. Stony Point. Dassen Island.

1

The parents, jostled
by a surging storm
lost the dream
of feeding him,
the sea-vein broken,
and in evening light
the deep promises
no possible solution.
Darkness falls,
soft and quiet.

2

Flung from its nest
dressed in pyjamas
of snowy feathers,
with soft penguin peeps
and little oars flapping,
the bird-child lies
in the hand of the vet,
hungry as a room.
its open beak wanting
more and more tiny
sardine pieces.

We Came for the Whales

We didn't come for the limpets
tending their sea gardens,

or the sea anemones wearing
mad shells on their heads,

sheltering from the sunlight,
we came for the whales,

the southern rights and humpbacks,
bodies as big as boats,

breaching and tail slapping
wallowing with their newborns

in the shallow waters
just beyond the breaking surf.

Arriving, the sun hardly risen,
the tide having rolled back,

we were on our knees, our faces and hair
reflected in lost whirlpools

of underwater worlds,
light pools in which Sirius glitters,

where jellyfish shift as clouds.
We discovered ancient fish traps,

middens, uncovered by the washing tide,
tiny fish and periwinkles,

studded rocks draped with seaweed,
the whales forgotten,

until the tide came in,
closed like a fist.

Two Birds

Two little birds flew in
one perfect day when
the doors stood open;
one flew off, the other
stayed, hopped from
kettle to fridge, from
shelf to table, then the
sound of wings on glass,
feathers flying, as it tried
to exit a closed window.

Not wanting to frighten,
I let it be, wrote a poem
as I watched, thinking
it would find its way,
feel the breeze of the open
door, but it flew around, noisy
and anxious, flinging its little
bird body against the pane,
making terrified bird noises.

Till I walked towards the tiny
quivering, guided the bundle,
shepherded it back into
a brighter light.

Aria

In Walker Bay a year ago to watch
southern rights coming close in,

I heard him before I saw him,
standing, with dark glasses, his back

to the water. He'd put his bike down
and, cap in hand, started singing

an aria from *La Boheme*, his voice
rising to take ownership of the street.

Everyone stopped in their tracks,
then clapping and whistling as he

jumped back on his bike and pedalled away.
The whales kept diving and surfacing.

Earthward

I found the place and stayed.
Unlike the hadedas who flew
off to the horizon, frightened
by whipping winds,
the caracals lurking.
The eagle owl is here too,
and nightjars in the dunes.

I get to feel the touch of sea,
the oily perfume of bush,
the sandy road that suddenly
becomes an ocean, cutting off
the world and people. I listen

in bodiless moments to the sounds
of night, and love the heavy pulse
of gathered earth, dove's feet
on the tin roof, black-eyed birds bathing,
the solitude, an acquired sweetness.

Men found it, too, cocksure
of breaking ground, stealing
sunshine, the moon blue
and haunting, its godlike
silence. Stones and grit,
ancient wood gnarled
as works of art, each still
in its own rightful place.

Messenger

The dull thud was not the noon cannon
on Signal Hill, but a dove that had crashed
into my window. It lay on its back for a while,
feet in the air, tried first one wing and then
the other to see if they worked, and suddenly

silently died. The vision of the open space
behind was not what it seemed,
and colliding with the gleam of light
the image brought only darkness.

Noah sent a dove to see if the waters
had subsided, and when it returned
he knew, knew the land was still
a never-ending sea. The closing
of a window, the opening of another,
I sat awhile in the sun, contemplated
our drowning.

Oracle

I knew all along we were walking
over an underground lake, never
wondered whether the wetness

beneath had played with the sand,
created muddied cities of ancient
shells and castles under our feet,

prehistoric fish and the ghosts
of the oldest men living in
the darkest underworld.

But when the messenger of God
lay dead on my stoep, I knew.
The old rivers of life had shifted,

little rivulets that once flowed
had sunk, boreholes dried up,
our lives of plenty ended.

On the Stoep

They have gone, and dinner alone
is stranger than the sudden heat,
the ominous shimmering, and me
hosing the bush around the house,
useless, but soothing to the nerves.

The sugar birds in and out
of the newly filled bird bath,
darting here, there, knowing
it's the only thing to do.

The wind dropped, the evening turned
beautiful, my unease not diminished
by silence, clouds erupting unexpectedly,
relief, knowing the scorching will not last.

The weight of my thoughts, like plants
disturbed, needing to settle. A little food,
perhaps a glass of wine, the pen lies
on the table, a fan of pages.

Encounter

I spotted them from a distance,
a woman, a man, a row of clothes,
the small house, the day as hot
as yesterday. They were the first

I had come across after hours of hiking,
the woman's misty eyes, the way
her son danced, the movement
a blossoming, reaching inward

to an imagined core, weightless
and untouchable, heads turned
upward, their lives uninterrupted
by any knowledge or any book.

As natural as earth and air, never
hiding the fountain of themselves,
they are the caretakers of a coastline.

The Iconic Southernmost Tip of Africa Builds a New Monument

Arrows point east and west where the two oceans meet,
Atlantic and Indian on rocks like needles;
cold and warm lovers that crash as they greet.

Cameras aim at the sea as it ceaselessly beats-
can they really see where the oceans mingle?
Arrows point east and west where two oceans meet.

Rocks are piled for foundations-near complete-
a structure to impose, like the local fish eagle,
where cold and warm lovers must crash as they greet.

But old stones are not grand, and they want concrete,
while the fish couldn't care, nor the gulls and the beetles.
Cold and warm oceans just butt heads and greet.

From all over the world, they have come in the heat,
the winding new boardwalk is easy and neat;
arrows point east and west where two oceans meet.

No view undiscovered, natural feels obsolete,
there's nowhere to hide on this shore, no retreat.
Arrows point east and west where the two oceans meet,
cold and warm lovers that crash as they greet.

Essence

The sparseness. Faded crimson
curtain pulled to the side, a dulled
evening light, wilted petals on the table,
books lying on the Persian rug.
I've kept this photo like the winter tree,
undressed in cold, shrouded as a cloud,
colour wiped clean.
This unravelling will surely unearth
what is real: soil and air, rain and sun,
a faded disparate beauty, nothing but itself.

PART TWO

Cicadas

The cicadas in the trees above
have been making that sharp singing
sound all day, starting and stopping
taking a rest, and then an explosion
of noise, as if trying to drown our voices
in the kitchen, and it has just occurred
to me standing at the window, washing
the breakfast cups, that their lives
depend on their singing, unseen
but constant and that this is the heart's
greatest project:
                       learning how to hold on,
to keep on trying to make something
of the bright new surface of each day,
and at the same time recognise
and cherish the great scar of demise.

To live with desire for both, to know
their names, and as the cicadas, sing
out an endless call in the heat of summer,
and when the damp cold winds blow,
return underground, to sip
sap from the roots of trees.

Borderlines

If I would paint the dense flow
of hills, summer burnt brown,

the silver olive and old cypress,
my brush would be a thinking body

as it moved from branch to leaf,
a movement of dark gorges

and lighter spirals; my skin tingling,
the body in unity of being.

This silent landscape imposes
its ideas on mine, borderlands

of forests and slanting meadows
all crowd boldly, a broken illusion

in the dizzy heat. The final touch,
the painting is whole,

the spell broken.

Abandoned in Tuscany

She was a beauty once,
her walls frescoed
with classical scenes
but now, the sun of summers
having done its work,
layers peel away
as she slowly crumbles,
lungs filling with dust,
the arched door's lock
rusting solid.
The rooms are full
of nondescript boxes.
The old-eye windows
are dim and empty.

Turning Point

At their most vulnerable,
open and naked to the world
on this day in January.

Beeches and oaks, pines
at the top of the hill,
their quiet meeting
with a loaded sky.

Do we reach a point
when we can no longer?
A spine, fragile and weak,
waiting for the season to turn
we glimpse a limping sun
and look beyond.

I remember childhood days
when we dived into mountain pools,
reached the muddy bottom, and
turned our bodies upward,
weightless arms unfurled,
swimming from the bottom
of the world, towards light.

Day in the Veluwe

They appeared as vague pale shapes
in morning, the sun not yet declared,

the grass a wet mat of sod and root
hooked to the earth by scraps of webs,

the sheep pressing against the fence,
billowing forms, then later thinning,

the dog barking outside the flock,
the sheep moving to the end

of the meadow, then back again,
a narrow pathway beneath

the fallen sky as I watched
the long-tailed sheep enclosed

in their small silver chamber,
low-country sheep, earthy and real,

my feet slipping in ooze,
the shepherd eating bread

as he kept watch for the wolf,
around but not yet seen.

A closed existence, waiting
for the sun to come to light.

The Garden Next Door

is being properly dressed,
soft earth turned, all the nettles
thistle, silky windgrass and mustard
still blooming but dug up, jewel weeds
that blew into this lost Eden.

Straight rows, now organised;
the feral rose-ringed parakeets
scream on, undisturbed, flap
and cry out, their wings,
the colour of green glass
blend with the new grass mats
being put in place.

Look at the trees,
where light touches umber,
the bend of trunks,
their quiet standing,
the way old oaks fall,
let go, moss growing.

I pace the fence between us,
barefooted, tread the earth,
small clusters of bindweed,
dandelion and evening primrose
thrive just outside my door,
nothing changed.

I'm going to keep things like this!

Chestnut in Winter

Niet vallen, kijk uit.
Five small children
high in the branches,
laughing, shouting,
their thin bodies climb

and whirl, concentration
on their faces, intent,
without fear, their games
seem to have some reason.

Monstrous battles, secret
betrayals in the forest,
brutal deaths, and when
they return to the classroom
their drawings will be
of swords and explosions.

The old tree is crumbling under
the attack of small feet and hands,
thick waisted, split down the middle.

PART THREE

Sunday Morning in Paris

The winter snow has melted, leaving a chilled pool on the ping pong table in the park. Mr Hautamaki and Mrs Bellerose carefully scrape away the puddle. She takes off her coat, bared arms in the park on this chilly morning. The oriental gentleman has been practising, hitting the little ball high into the greyness, again and again. My eye follows its quickness to where spinning hands open. To where the ball flies across the table. Back and forth, back and forth – to him to her. Keep it up, one slip and you are lost! Sunlight shifts, cat like across the park. Late morning shadows now lengthen, as the opponents sense in each other, as in the April earth, a seed awakening.

A Street in Amsterdam

A young waiter with tied back hair has stepped out of the Italian pizza joint and is pointing out an attraction to a tourist. Later in the same street a young woman in a ball gown walks in the rain. The woman drops her stola in front of the pizza joint and stooping to pick it up she catches sight of the waiter smoking a cigarette. The woman and waiter twirl for a moment on the wet pavement. The sudden encounter has caused a resonance. The pitter patter of rain jounces with their warm bodies. A tick, a purr, a drop. The light of the street lantern turns red, turns golden.

It Will Happen

he said softly in the morning
after the night's rain. Darkness

was long and a slow morning
opened. They survived the deluge

and the wind that moved as if
at war. Ants were on the move,

a newly born spider, two centipedes
entangled for hours were curled

into each other, and the sky washed out
as perlemoen clouds drifted.

Not knowing what he meant.
Only a yearning, the beekeeper

and his love; the wings of his bees
pulsing in shafts of sunlight.

A Look at Love

Now that they have fallen out of shadow,
they are seeing things afresh,

a chrysalis emerging, transparent
as shiny drops, clothed in shimmering.

This weightless day breaks
to the stranger's they have become,

the silence as palpable as smoke;
they turn to each other. Bodies

bound by threads of silk, together
though apart. Plumed wings unfolding.

Embrace

Rodin travelled to Carrara
to find a block of veinless marble

to carve his Kiss – smoothness
worked into skin, folded

into night, the embrace
a doorway to elation.

Bones, muscles and nerves,
the clay shrunk once during firing,

this time his hand not quite on her thigh,
the spiral composition of a forbidden love,

sinners drifting in the wind, his mouth
set on hers, bodies intertwined.

And the tiny replicas on the panel,
Paola and Francesca kiss

at the Gates of Hell.

My Father's Heart

My father is a fisherman,
he sits in the prow of the boat,
facing the shore, as restless
as the sea today.

A big-bellied man,
he loves to joke.
He takes me across,
helps me ashore.

We talk of what lies deeper,
the wonder of anemones,
urchins and starfish,
and I tell him how I used to dive
that antipodean world
in turbulent times.

He had a great love of the sea,
so we slowly strew him
in the wind of the Bay,
taken by the cold Benguela,
seeing him gently folded
into its great cold blanket.

He always insisted
on staying above water,
never swam or took
the plunge to the deep
rich bed of ocean,

the underwater heart
of his loved one,
for, as a true vessel,
he held the sea within him.

Ode to Legs

And where will you take me,
you who have led me into being?

Femur, tibia, fibula and patella,
you who grew in my seventh week,

that became legs, sturdy and strong,
you that take your job seriously.

How precious you are, dancing
and jumping for joy just as a caracal

that swats a flying bird in the air,
opening to celebrate life and great pleasure,

thank you for your flower walk,
the unrolling of the carpet,

you have never let me down.
Shake a leg, never a tail between legs,

get a leg up, garters and stilettos, red
furry slippers, stockinged silk, you

are me, right down to my naked feet.
We take on the earth, are part

of the soil, take me to the far corners,
for a walk on the wild side.

The Wife of my Ex

This is the house of the wife
of my ex-lover.
She lives on a drifting island,
from her I borrow novels,
nothing is mine.
My ex is the sort of man
who wouldn't hurt a fly,
she has a swatter.
Love comes in waves,
like the ocean, a sickness
which grows, she has no bandages,
a raw voice, she is everywhere.
With him she plays musical chairs,
he is glad not to be left out,
I am the seat of elimination,
I know she does not
like me to play.

Image

I can see them:
the young woman
and two little ones,
climbing over her,
pulling her hair,
jumping on her lap,
diving into cushions
on the chair. I watch
on screen, little voices,
childish excitement.

She moves away, trying
to keep up conversation -
in my mind I see
a lioness and her cubs
in the Kruger Park.
Purrs and love bites,
they scramble for her
attention, wrestle with her,
it's a game, she's the prey.

The image blurs,
she lets out a roar.
A hot wind rushing through
her blonde mane, as if
this mother has met
her beginning, turned
the colour of earth.

A Child Plays

A little girl plays, intent,
loose spine and silky limbs,
sleek and wild, filled with gladness.
Is this what Rousseau meant:
no sin nature, happiness
an inside job, little body
lit up, shaking with pleasure,
the world just that moment,
hung in her game like a heart.

PART FOUR

PART FOUR

Kaggen, the Thief of Time

It's ten p.m. and Sylvia puts on
the red dress she wore so long ago,
conjures her man to her side,
blows out the wind-flickered
candle flame as the sound
of his voice washes over.

She smiles as she remembers:
two people sit at a table,
shadow shapes playing into
each other, eyes closed,
each with no purpose except
to move together, to have
the kind of intactness
of living mirrors.

Years have lurched through a veil
of time – it's almost midnight.
Sylvia collects her thoughts,
sets herself against the chill
of her man's ghost when
Kaggen suddenly appears,
says he can recognise Sylvia's
shadow as her life shimmers
in the periphery of light and pall.

Kaggen points out the outline
of a wooden sculpture in the half dark,
its soft curves she has never noticed,
taking her back, back so far
she can barely remember....

ஓ

He was young and dapper, reminds Kaggen,
standing in a draughty entrance,
the cold unheeded, holding roses
and unanswerable questions.

Hands as soft as powder, as falling
sand in an hourglass, Sylvia remembers
her man's night fingers, fluttering
and drunk from the fragrance of oil.

My hands were trapped in the neck of a tortoise,
says Kaggen, his image slowly dissolving,
*and when it drew in its head
nothing was left of my skin and nails.*

ஓ

Her man discovered the navel of her world,
together they held a ceremony of dreams,
though his words were made of air.
As the inside of an ancient cave,
where on the vault of rock a cloud
of palms have been painted, delicate swarms

holding sealed messages.

Kaggen is close again and Sylvia
recalls: two pairs of lips closing,
slowly drawing in on each other,
alive but not real, they are caught
in the brightness of their imaginations.

It seems eons that they have circled each other,
*As the ancient myth of the hare cursed
by the moon, not able to rebuff death,
forever hounded by the wild dog*, nods Kaggen.

The candle now spluttering, moonlight shivering,
everything leading to her and her man
foundering into each other, Sylvia knows
she has touched the slender shadow line.

Kaggen relates the story of the broken string,
a sacred chain carrying messages,
like strings of letters lying yellowed
as a lifetime of fallen leaves.

*But remember the broken string
brings death*, says Kaggen,
a heart fallen from the throat
dies on parched earth.

Red coral, jade, tiger's eye;

her man gave her none of these,
just a simple leather cord
from an unknown country.

All summer long Sylvia waited,
the pale shimmer of a phosphorescent sea,
shorelines edged with rocks and reefs
and further aloe bushes.

Not surrendering to loneliness
she woke to the scent of the ocean,
the little lip of wave that flattened
and spread out softly.

We were the surgeons of our hearts, she thinks
undertakers of our interiors,
and, resigned to live with a few tender things,
she hovered as a small bird.

The wagtail wears a dark choker,
its image painted in damp caves
centuries ago. Bushmen artists
remembered the tiny birds when
they saved their people by devouring
swarms of sand flies, said Kaggen.

༺

The years lurch through a veil of time,
as frail branches holding two bodies.
Sylvia remembers the blur of her man's limbs,

and the beat of heart and drum.
The green marula tree, the baobab,
the golden mopane glistens in morning,
all strings of images reflecting thoughts,
a small slice of African bush she put under
her pillow as a piece of wedding cake.

The stars say "Tsau Tsau", says Kaggen
*they steal your heart and it opens
like a flower in the sky.*

Sylvia's heart was thrown to the stars,
burned in the night, a wild landscape
cohabitating with the moon, smouldering
in light; the amber of a moment.

Sylvia is at the kitchen table
following a luminous trail,
a path through ribbons
of misalignment, a rough space
that is never empty.

*The right one but the wrong time
tricks the heart, is the greatest
shape shifter*, points out Kaggen.

࿊

It's afternoon and three ostriches,
heads down, are foraging for food,
the day's heat cuts as a knife.

Sylvia shadow dances with ghosts,
heeds Kaggen as he tells of his vision,
the last Bushman song sung into the night;
between worlds Sylvia waits for the evening star,
and the gibbous moon which will rise again.

NOTES

Page 11   Overberg: A region east of Cape Town

Page 21   Stoep: Veranda

Page 33   Veluwe: A national park in the Netherlands

Page 35   Kijk uit niet vallen: Look out, don't fall!

Page 59   *Kaggen the Thief of Time*: The poetry collected from the Bushmen informants in the second half of the nineteenth century by Wilhelm Bleek and Lucy Lloyd, now in the Cape Town University Library, was used in this poem.

I am grateful to Douglas Reid Skinner for his advice.